from the author

My Culture, My Gender, Me
Cassandra Jules Corrigan
Illustrated by Moe Butterfly
ISBN 978 1 83997 762 6
eISBN 978 1 83997 763 3

The Pronoun Book
She, He, They, and Me!
Cassandra Jules Corrigan
Illustrated by Jem Milton
ISBN 978 1 78775 957 2
eISBN 978 1 78775 958 9

The Gender Book
Girls, Boys, Non-binary, and Beyond
Cassandra Jules Corrigan
Illustrated by Jem Milton
ISBN 978 1 83997 710 7
eISBN 978 1 83997 711 4

First published in Great Britain in 2025 by Jessica Kingsley Publishers
An imprint of John Murray Press

1

Copyright © Cassandra Jules Corrigan 2025

The right of Cassandra Jules Corrigan to be identified as the Author
of the Work has been asserted by them in accordance with the
Copyright, Designs and Patents Act 1988.

Illustrations copyright © Moe Butterfly 2025
Front cover image source: Moe Butterfly

All rights reserved. No part of this publication may be reproduced,
stored in a retrieval system, or transmitted, in any form or by any
means without the prior written permission of the publisher, nor
be otherwise circulated in any form of binding or cover other than
that in which it is published and without a similar condition being
imposed on the subsequent purchaser.

The fonts, layout and overall design of this book have been prepared
according to dyslexia friendly principles. At JKP we aim to make our
books' content accessible to as many readers as possible.

A CIP catalogue record for this title is available from the British
Library and the Library of Congress

ISBN 978 1 80501 401 0
eISBN 978 1 80501 402 7

Printed and bound in China by Leo Paper Products Ltd

Jessica Kingsley Publishers' policy is to use papers that are natural,
renewable and recyclable products and made from wood grown in
sustainable forests. The logging and manufacturing processes are
expected to conform to the environmental regulations of the country
of origin.

Jessica Kingsley Publishers
Carmelite House
50 Victoria Embankment
London EC4Y 0DZ

www.jkp.com

John Murray Press
Part of Hodder & Stoughton Ltd
An Hachette Company

The authorised representative in the EEA is Hachette Ireland,
8 Castlecourt Centre, Dublin 15, D15 XTP3, Ireland (email: info@hbgi.ie)

MY HISTORY, MY GENDER, ME

Cassandra Jules Corrigan

Illustrated by Moe Butterfly

Jessica Kingsley Publishers
London and Philadelphia

Greetings, friend! Are you a boy or a girl? For some of you, this may be a simple question. For others, the answer may be more complicated.

Many people around the world are intersex and were born with characteristics that aren't easily defined as male or female.

Others may identify as transgender, meaning that they do not identify as the gender they were assigned at birth.

Some of those people identify as non-binary, meaning that they do not identify as male or female, but as something else entirely.

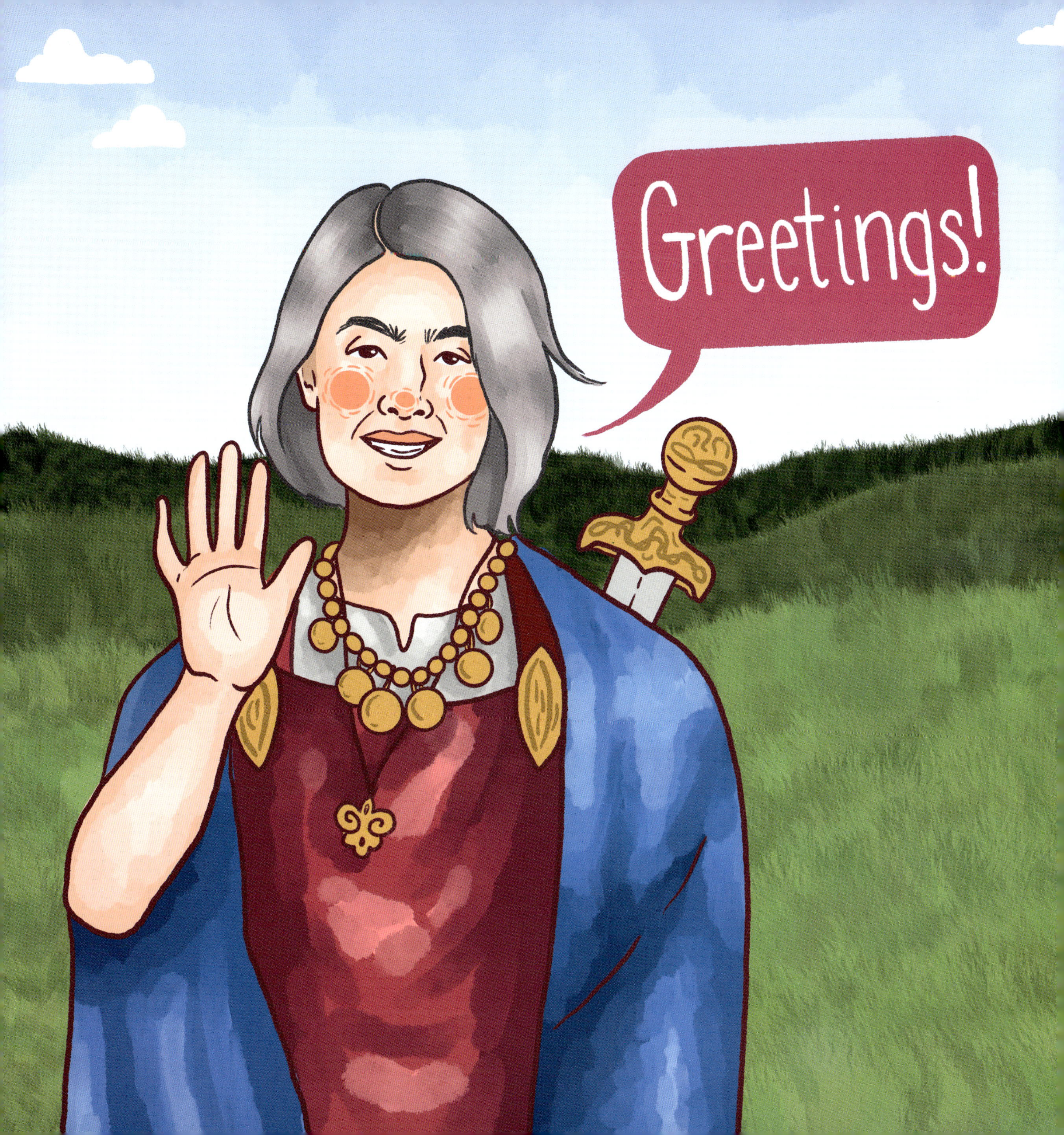
Greetings!

Many people know about non-binary, transgender, and intersex people today, but did you know that we have existed for thousands of years?

For example, I am known as the Suontaka (sahn-tah-kah) Person. I lived almost 1,000 years ago in Finland.

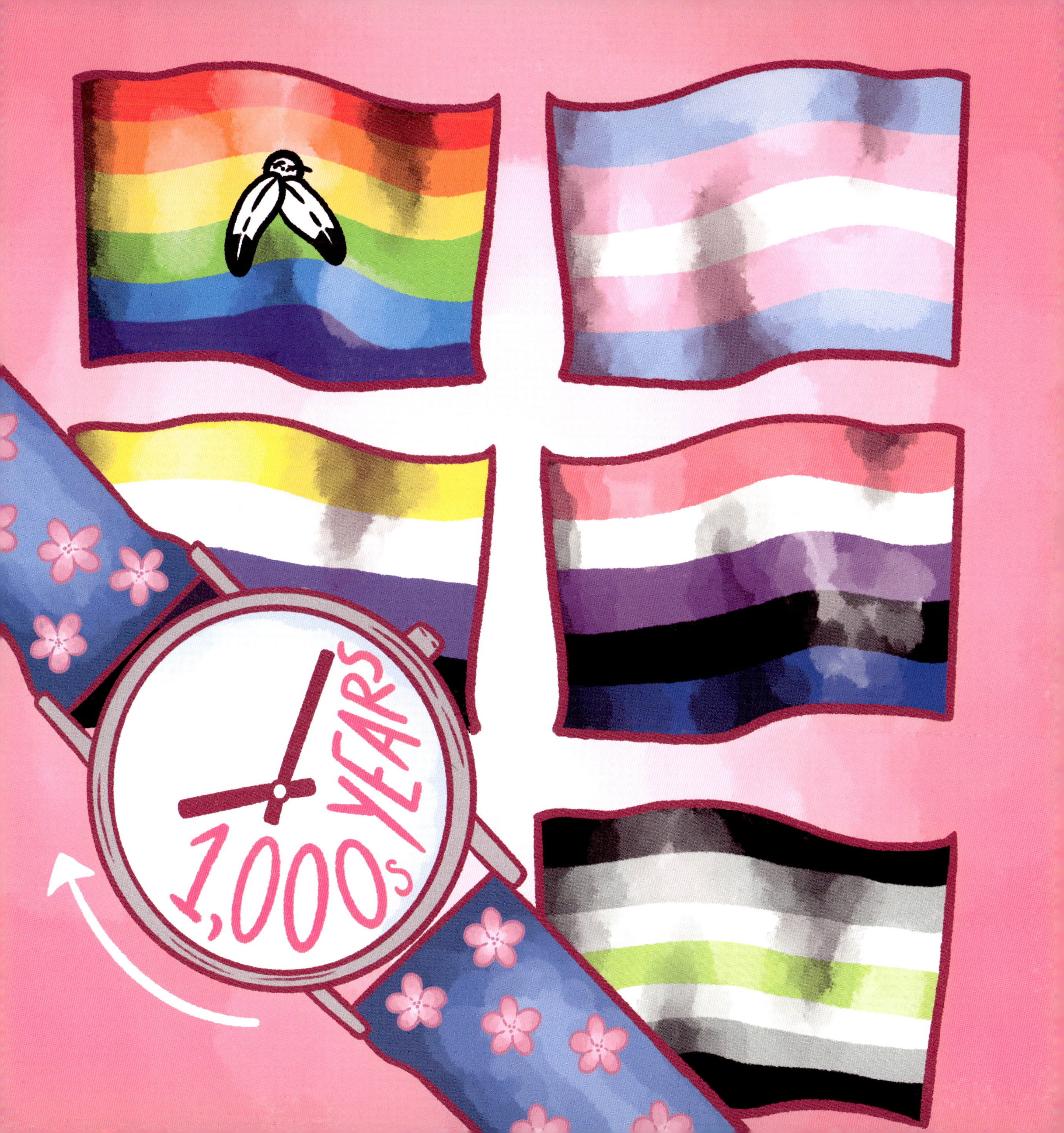
1,000s YEARS

After I died, I was buried with a sword, so I was probably a warrior in life. My grave was found by archeologists—people who study artifacts from history—in 1968.

At the time, they thought I was probably a woman, but scientists tested my DNA and discovered that I most likely had an intersex condition called Klinefelter syndrome, meaning that I had characteristics that were both male and female.

We now believe that it is possible that some Nordic people of non-binary genders or intersex conditions may have been highly respected in the Middle Ages.

Come along and read some more stories of people like me!

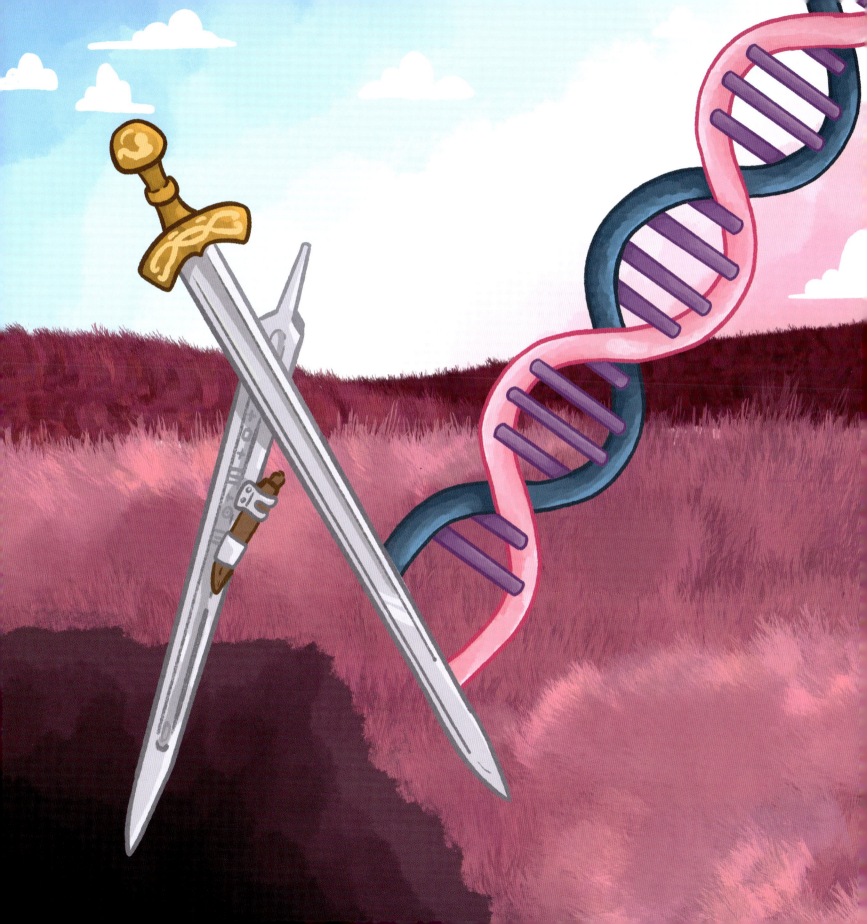

I am the Archigallus
(are-ki-gah-luhs).

I was the leader of the galli (gah-li) priests in Ancient Rome. The galli were a group of priests to the goddess Magna Mater, also known as Cybele (sib-ah-lee).

Our priesthood was comprised of people who were born men but adorned themselves with jewelry and makeup. Some historians believe that the galli were early examples of transgender women, and others see us as a third gender, entirely our own.

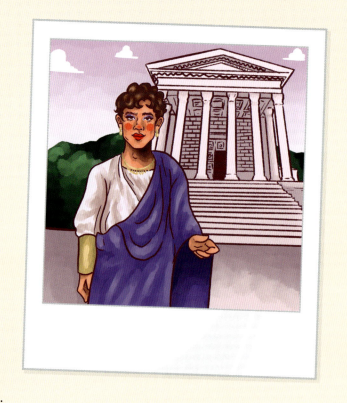

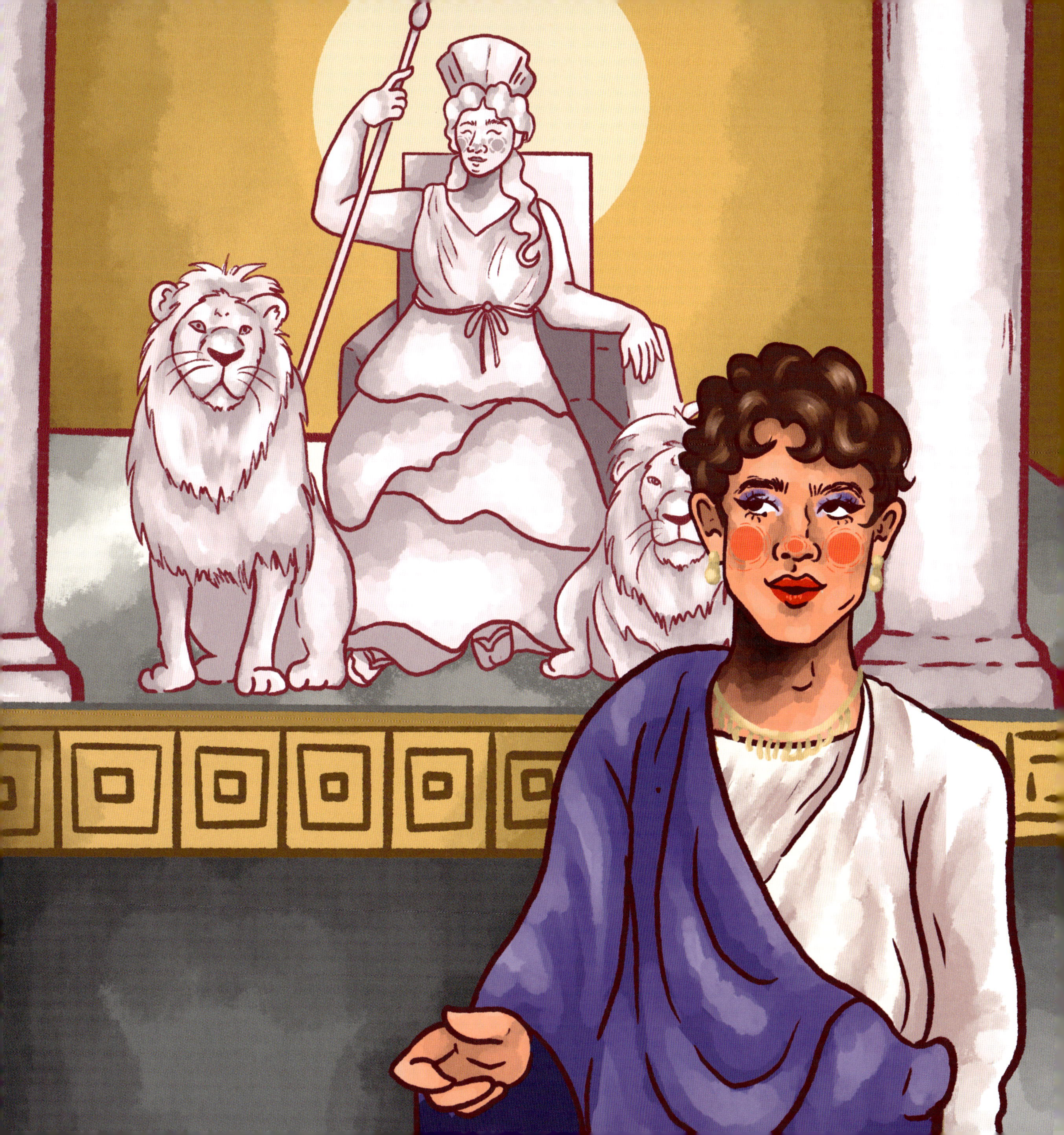

My name is Romaine-la-Prophétesse, or Romaine the Prophetess, and I was born in the island colony of Santo Domingo, in what is now Haiti, in the year 1750.

I was born as a free black person, and I believed that it was my divine duty to free slaves.

I soon became an early leader of the Haitian Revolution, and today researchers remember me as both an early example of transgender identity and a leader of folk religion when Haitian Vodou was new.

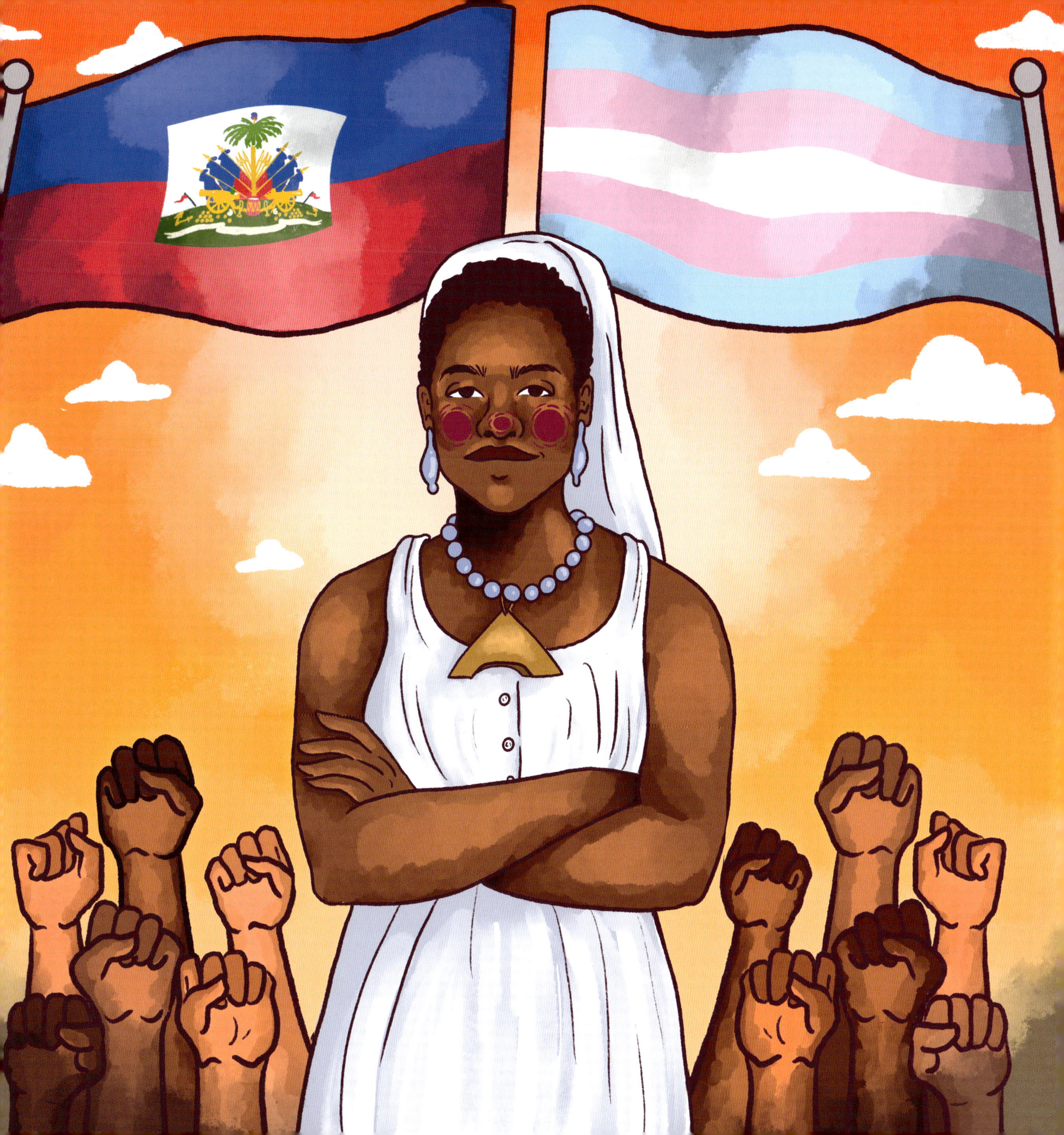

My name is Saint Marinos, although I am also known as Marina the Monk.

I was born in Lebanon in the 5th century and assigned female at birth.

I later joined a Christian monastery as a man, and my assigned gender at birth was not discovered until after my death.

Soon after, I was made a saint by both the Roman Catholic and the Eastern Orthodox churches. Today, I am proof that gender identity and religion do not have to be at odds.

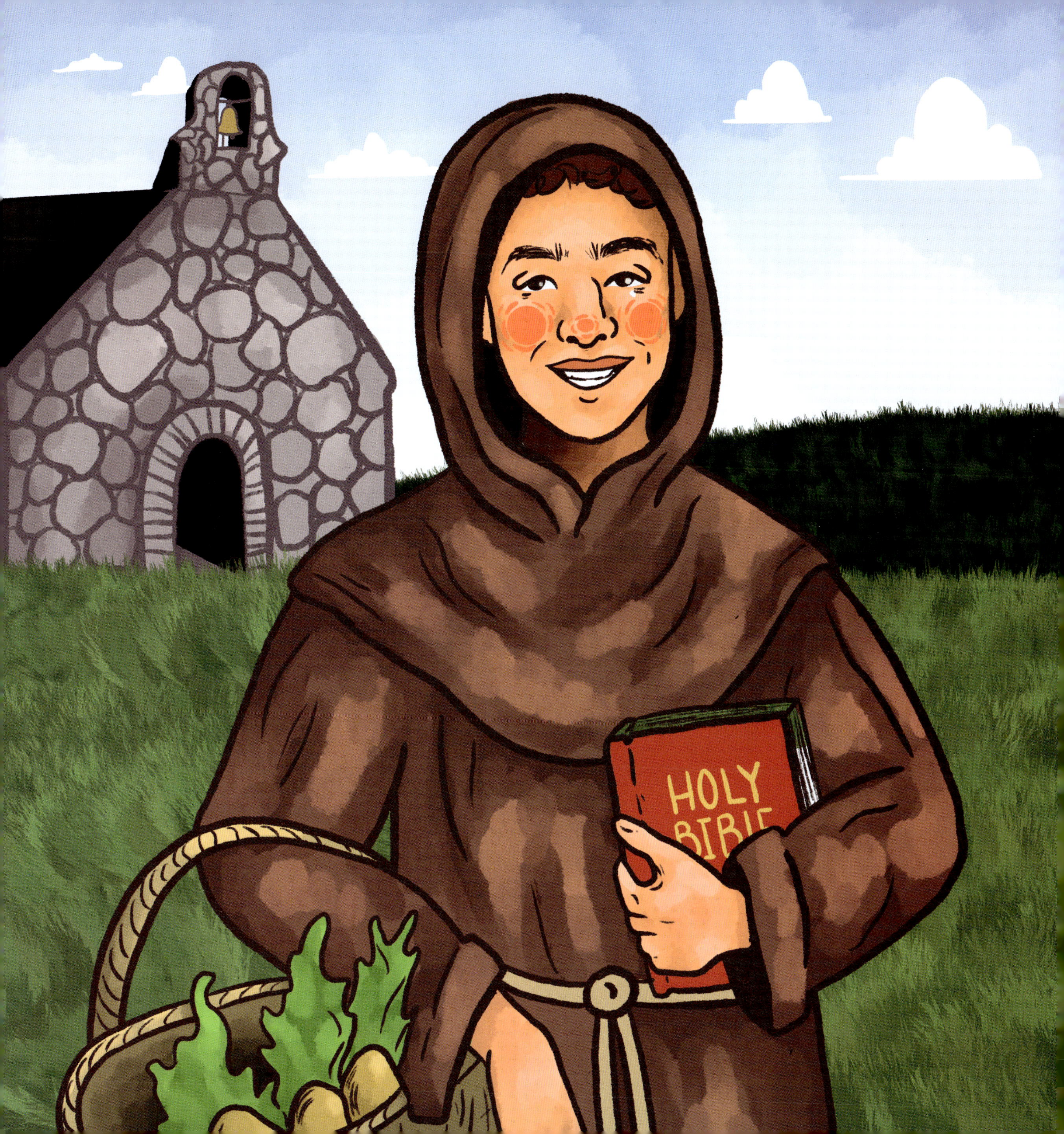
HOLY

My name is Lucy Hicks Anderson.

I was born in Appalachian Kentucky and assigned male at birth. But, as a young child, I renamed myself Lucy, and my parents decided to allow me to live as a transgender woman.

As an adult, I moved to California, and I married my husband Reuben in 1944, when it was illegal for two people who were assigned male at birth to be married.

When my assigned gender at birth was discovered by a doctor, I made history by choosing to go to prison rather than deny my marriage or my womanhood.

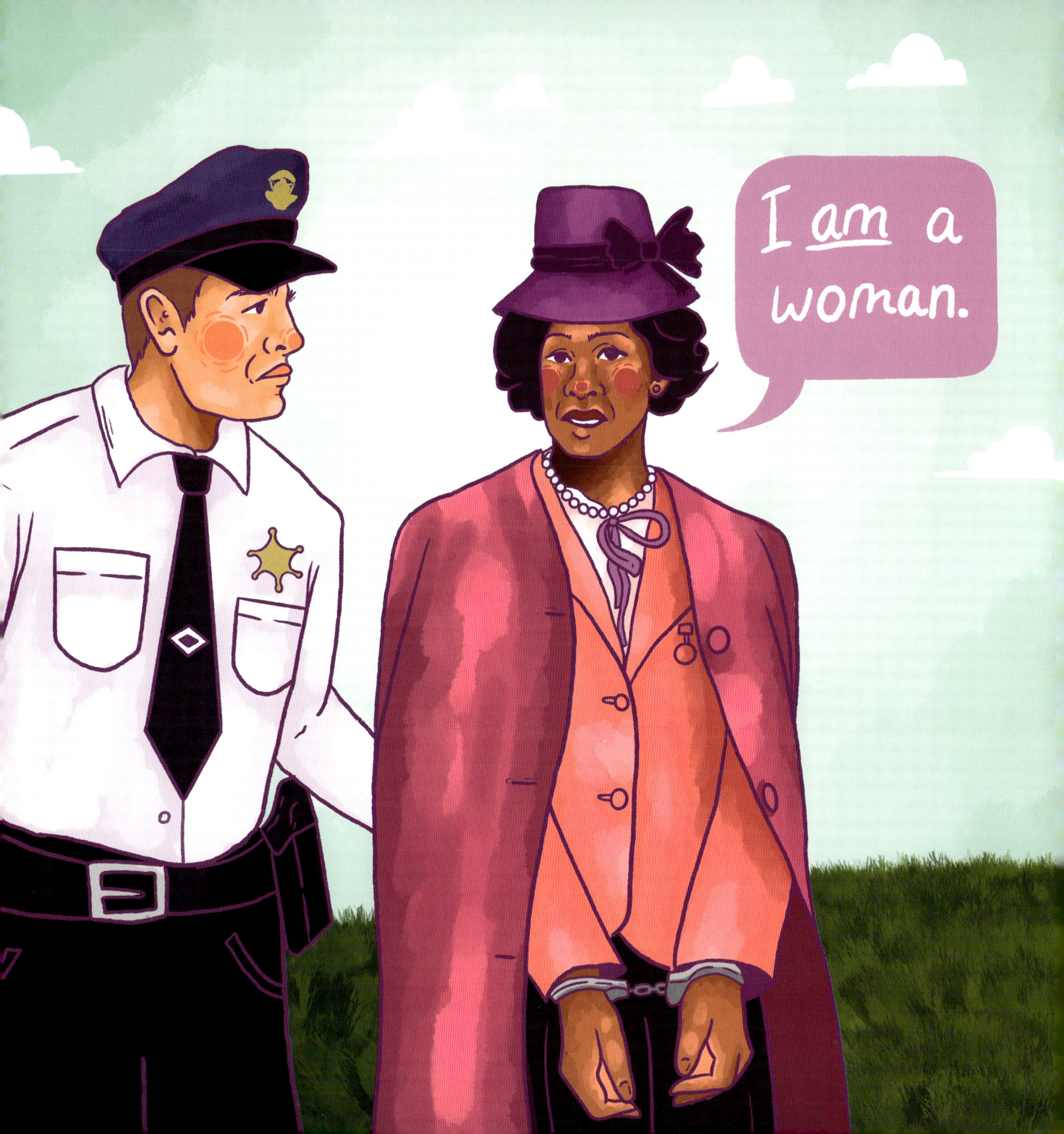
I am a woman.

My name is Marsha P. Johnson, and I was a trans woman. On June 28th 1969 I was at The Stonewall Inn, a gay bar in New York City.

At the time, being gay and dressing in clothes that society considered to be for a different gender was illegal in New York. That night, police raided The Stonewall Inn and began arresting and attacking everyone inside.

But my friends and I fought back and sparked a movement for rights for all LGBTQIA+ people. To this day, LGBT+ Pride Month is celebrated in June to remember the Stonewall Uprising.

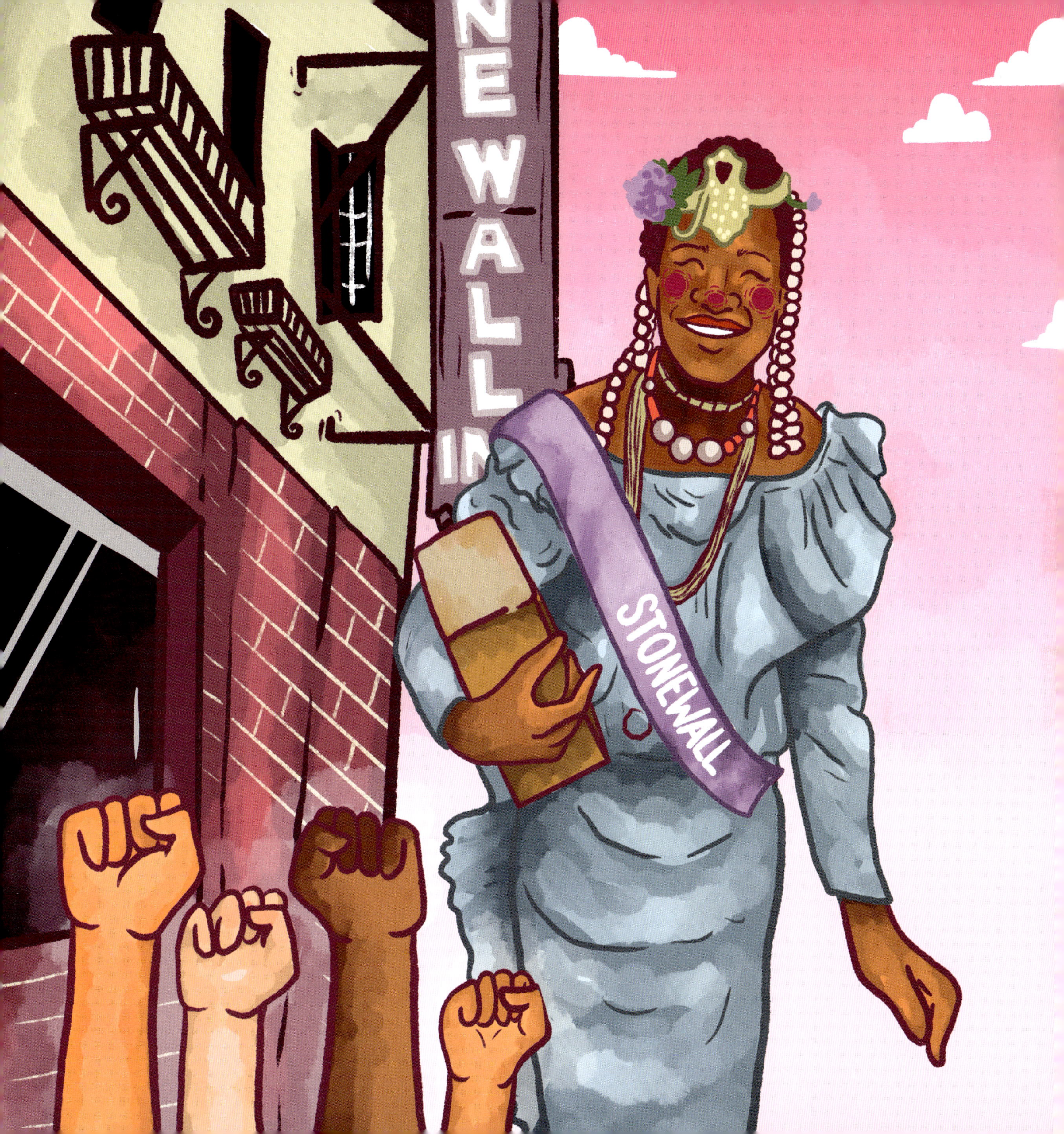
NEWALL IN
STONEWALL

My name is Dr. James Barry. I was born in Ireland in 1789 and went on to be a surgeon in the British Army.

I traveled all across the British Empire providing medical aid and performed one of the first caesarean sections where both the mother and baby survived.

I was an outspoken advocate for better living conditions for lepers, prisoners, and slaves, and I improved sanitation and clean water access in South Africa.

It was not until after my death that it was discovered that I was secretly a transgender man.

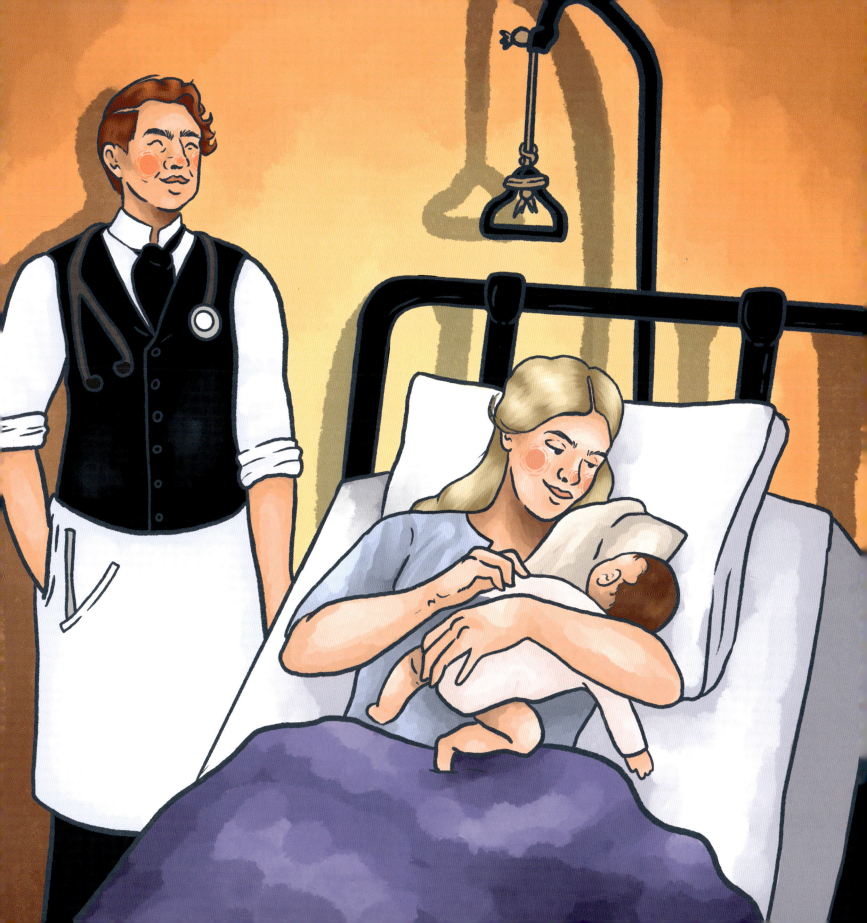

My name is We'wha (wee-wah). I was a member of the Zuni Native American community, born in 1849.

I was known as a lhamana (lah-ma-na), a cultural gender identity that today is sometimes included in the term Two Spirit.

I was a skilled craftsperson who became a cultural leader for my tribe, and my work was featured in the Smithsonian Institution and the National Theater.

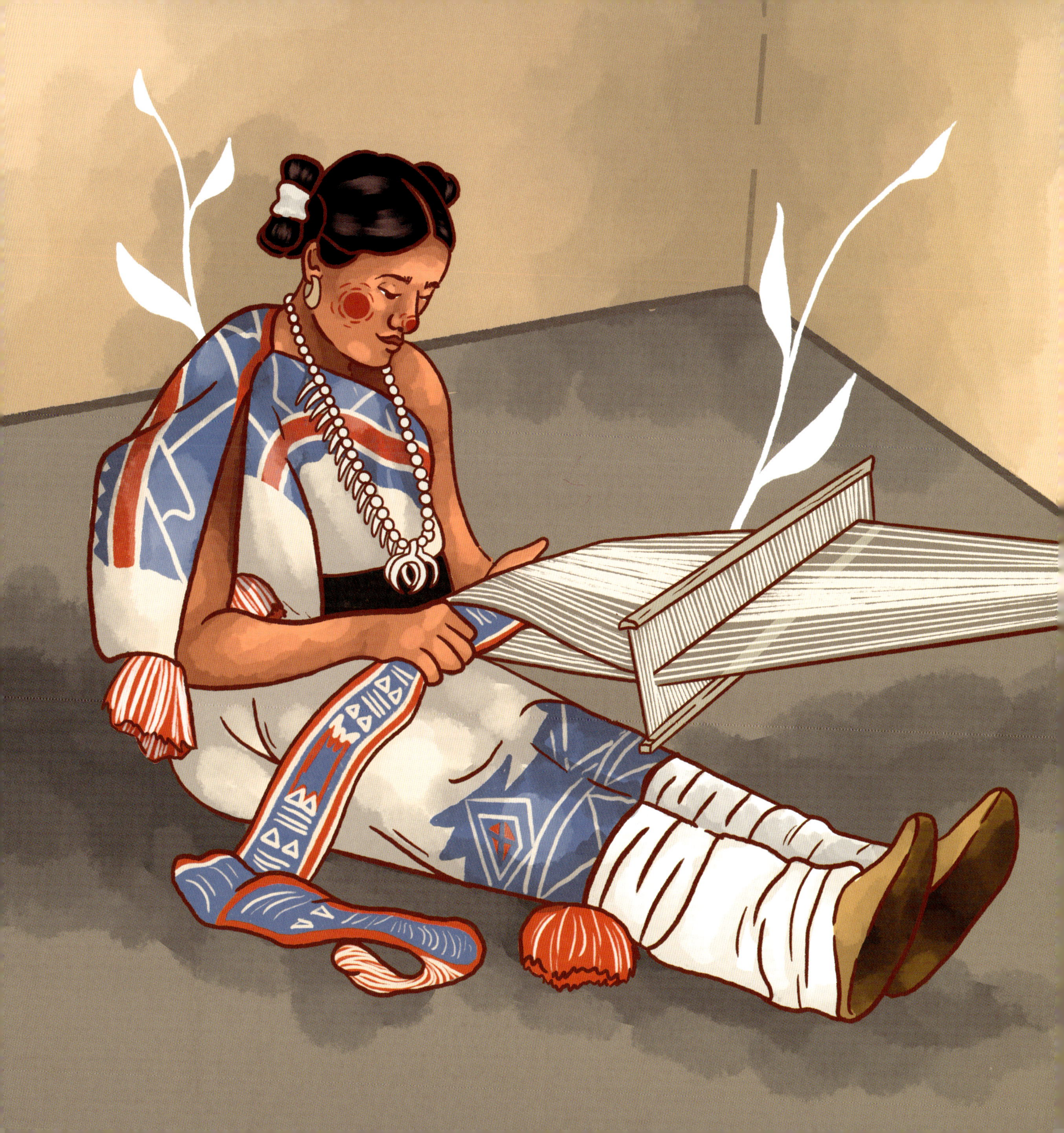

Hello! I am called the Public Universal Friend.

I was born as a woman to Quaker parents in 1752, but I later became a preacher and identified as genderless.

I taught hundreds of followers about my beliefs in free will and advocated for the end of slavery in America, peace with Indigenous peoples, and the rights of women.

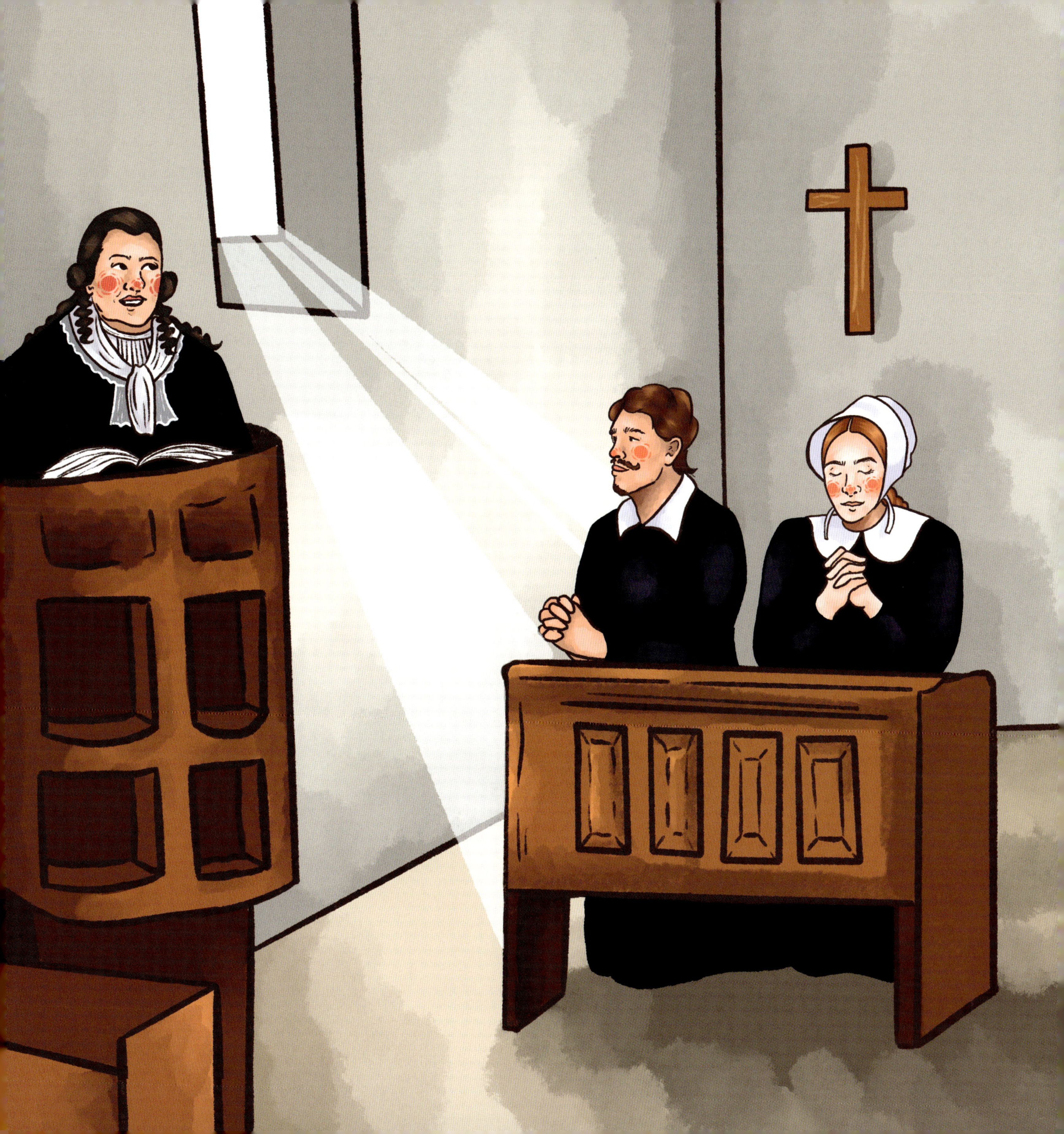

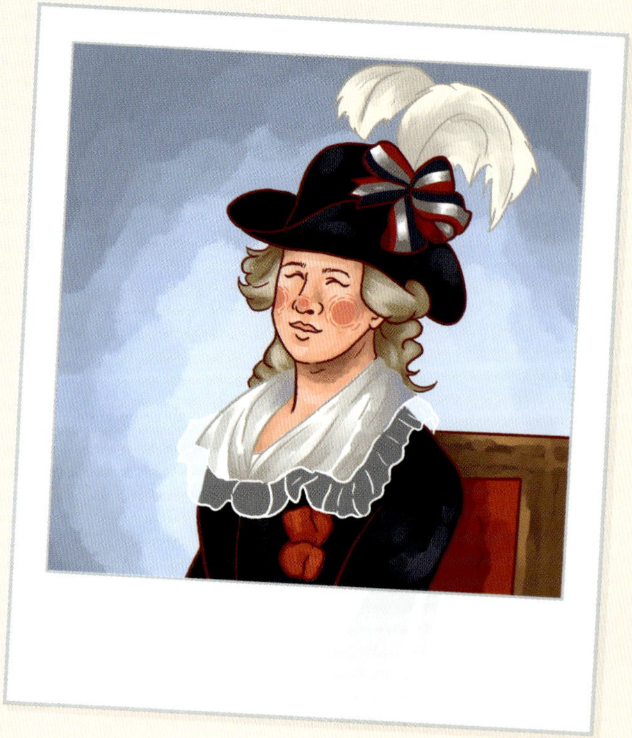

My name is Chevalier D'Eon. I was a spy for King Louis XV, as well as a soldier, and later a diplomat.

I spent time disguised as a maid in the court of Empress Elizabeth of Russia, but later decided to live the rest of my life as a woman.

I petitioned the government to recognize my gender as female and won.

Before the term "transgender" was commonly used, some people used "eonism" (ee-uh-ni-zim)—a word inspired by my name—to describe those who were born as one gender but lived as another.

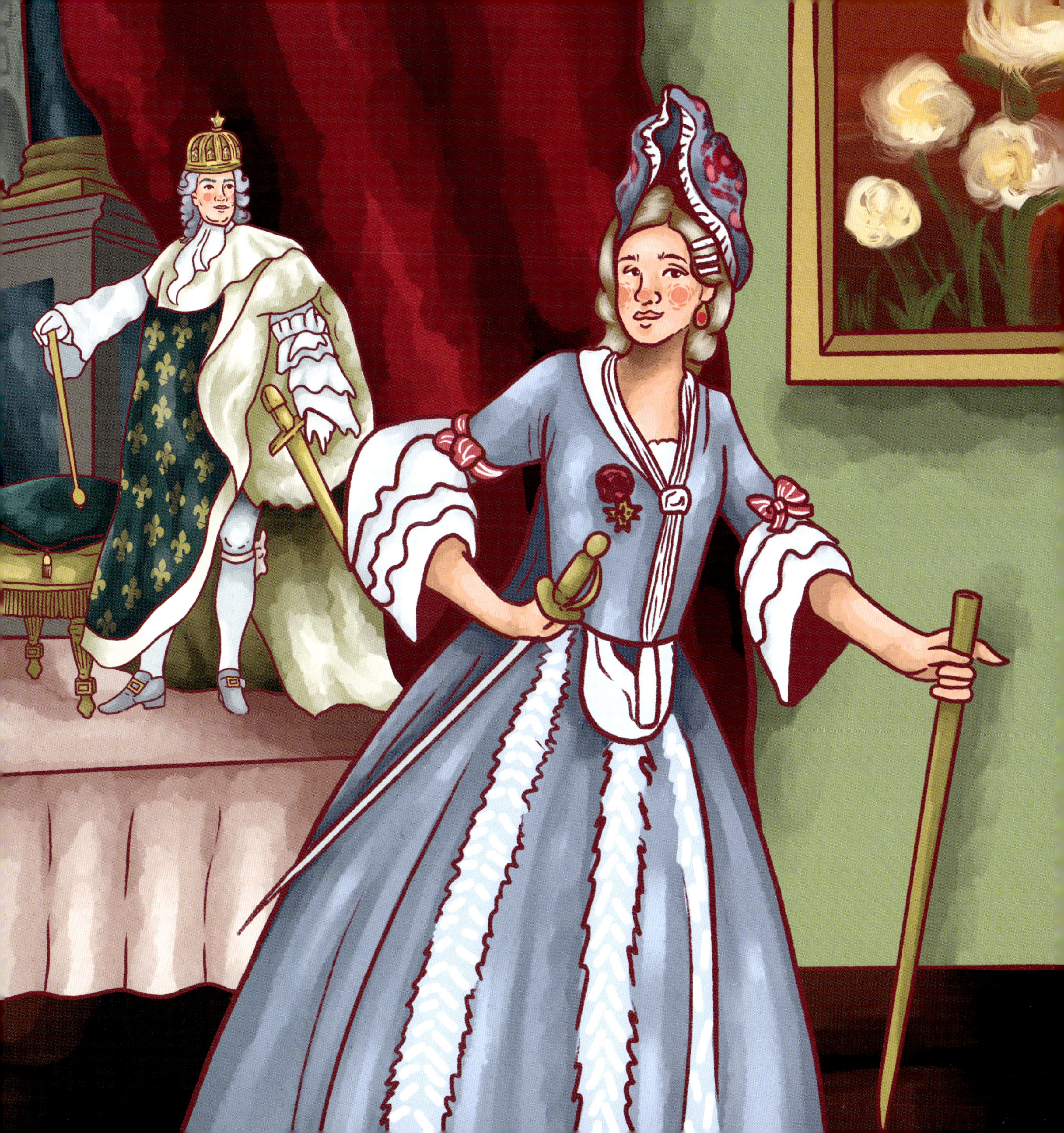

Isn't history incredible?

This is only a tiny portion of how diverse and vast our experiences can be.

But the best thing about history is that it never stops.

So, it's time to say goodbye and time for you to make history of your own.

The only question is, what will you do?

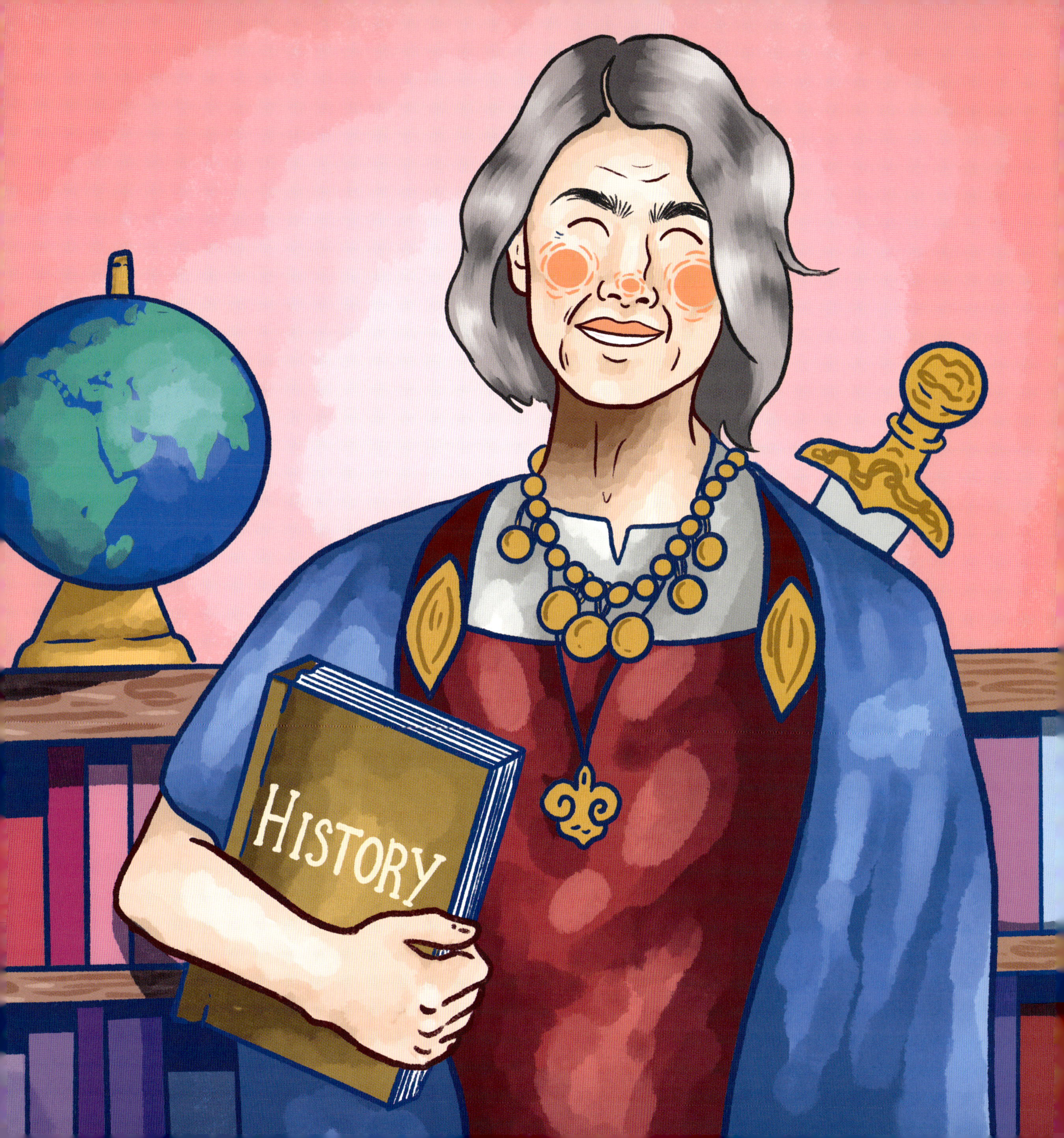
HISTORY

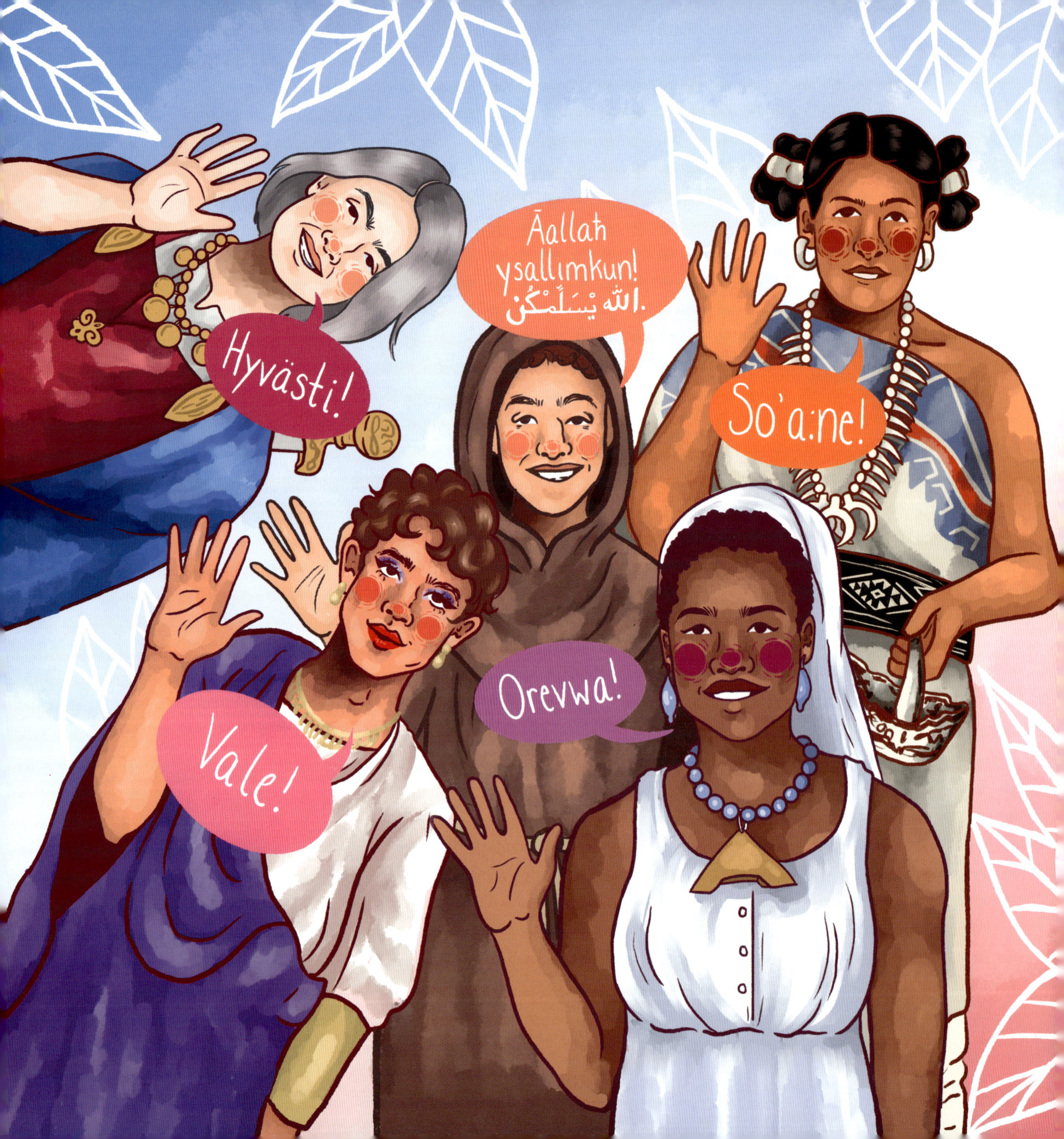
Hyvästi!
Āallaħ ysallimkun!
الله يْسَلِّمْكُنْ.
So'a:ne!
Vale!
Orevwa!

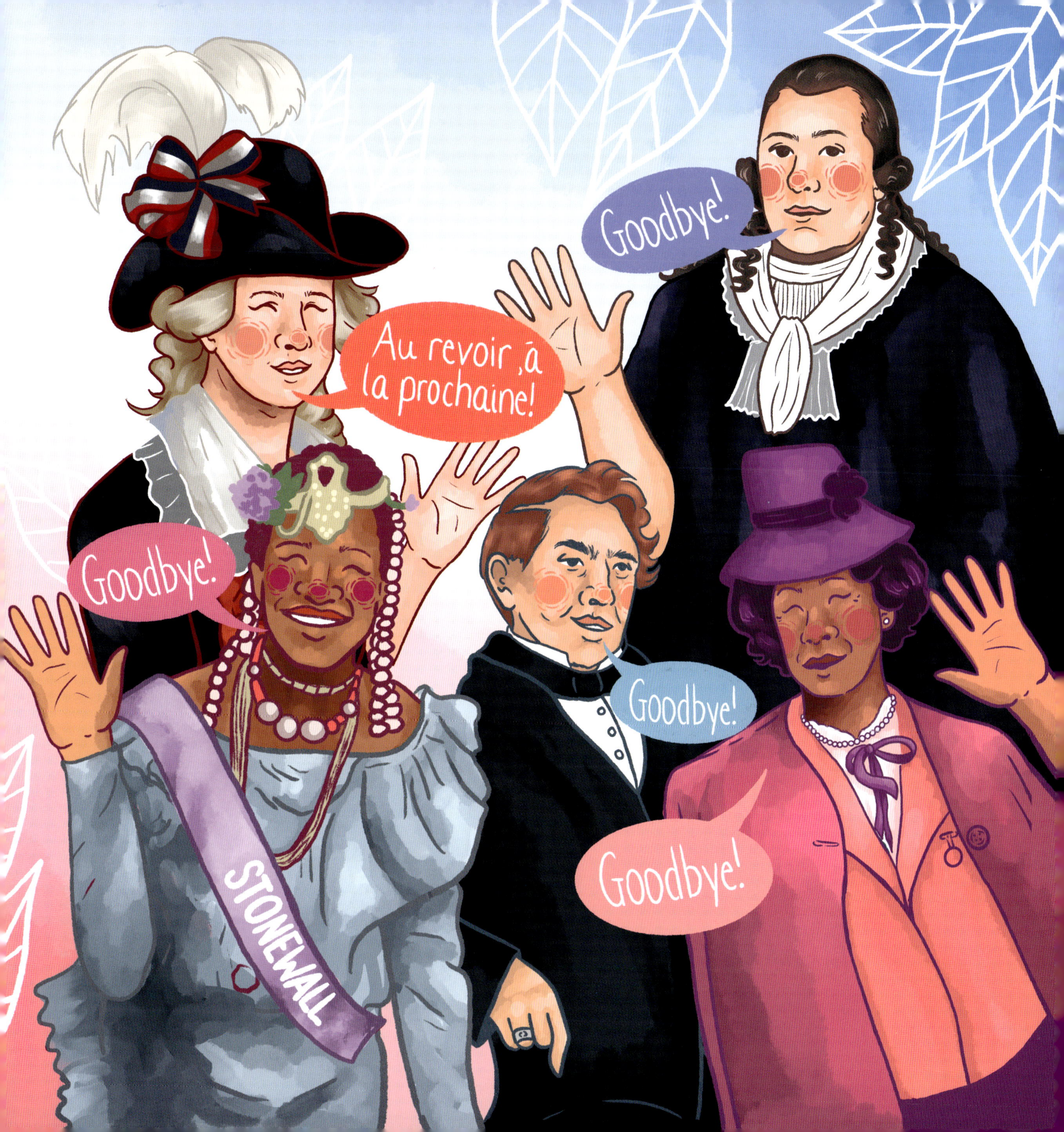
Goodbye!
Au revoir, à
la prochaine!
Goodbye!
STONEWALL
Goodbye!
Goodbye!

Author's note

I have been so honored to write about the diverse array of gender identities displayed in this book, but I would be remiss if I didn't mention a few things.

It's important to note that our current view of history is pieced together from bits of information that have survived from their time periods. As such, while we are always learning new things about history, there is also a lot we will never know about it, due to the way information and artifacts degrade or are destroyed over time.

This is to say, that it's entirely possible that other cultures not included in this book had their own words for trans, non-binary, and intersex individuals in their societies, but the records of that information may have been lost to time.

For example, one scholar suggested the existence of a third gender recognized in Ancient Egypt, known as "sekhet." However, the record of this proposed identity only exists from one source, so it's unclear if this third gender actually existed or if we are missing pieces of the story that would point to sekhet meaning something entirely different.

Additionally, history is written by the victors, so it's hard to accurately interpret stories from centuries or millennia, especially when it comes to gender and sexuality.

Some sources believe that we may have even had a trans Roman emperor named Elagabalus, but it's possible this was propaganda written after their death.

However, despite the passage of time, stories of queer people persist and can be found in every corner of history. While I didn't have enough space to include every one in this book, I encourage anyone who is interested in learning more to check their library or the internet with the supervision of a trusted adult. And if you are curious about where the particular stories I have chosen for this book come from, you can find a list of my sources on the JKP website here:
www.jkp.com/catalogue/book/9781805014010.

Finally, I want to thank you all for reading my writing and books like mine that showcase identities and histories that aren't always taught in schools.

Discussion questions

- Who was your favorite person to learn about in this book? Why?
- Some people in this book, like Lucy Hicks Anderson and Marsha P. Johnson, went through many struggles to be seen as the gender they identified with. What kind of struggles do you think transgender people go through today, and how have things gotten better since Lucy and Marsha were alive?
- People like We'wha probably lived in communities where being non-binary was considered as normal as being a boy or a girl. Do you think life was easier for them compared to people like Marsha? If so, how?
- Dr. James Barry hid his assigned gender at birth. Why do you think he did that?
- Some people in this book had strong religious beliefs. Do you have any religious beliefs? How do those beliefs (or lack thereof) influence how you see gender?
- Several cultures across the world featured androgynous priests who may have been non-binary. Why do you think that multiple cultures may have seen androgyny as something sacred?

Activity: Use your imagination!

Ask an adult for some paper and colored pencils. Draw or write about a trans, non-binary, or intersex person from history.

You can use one of the characters from this book as inspiration, or make up a story for a new character you invent!

What is their story and how does their identity influence them?

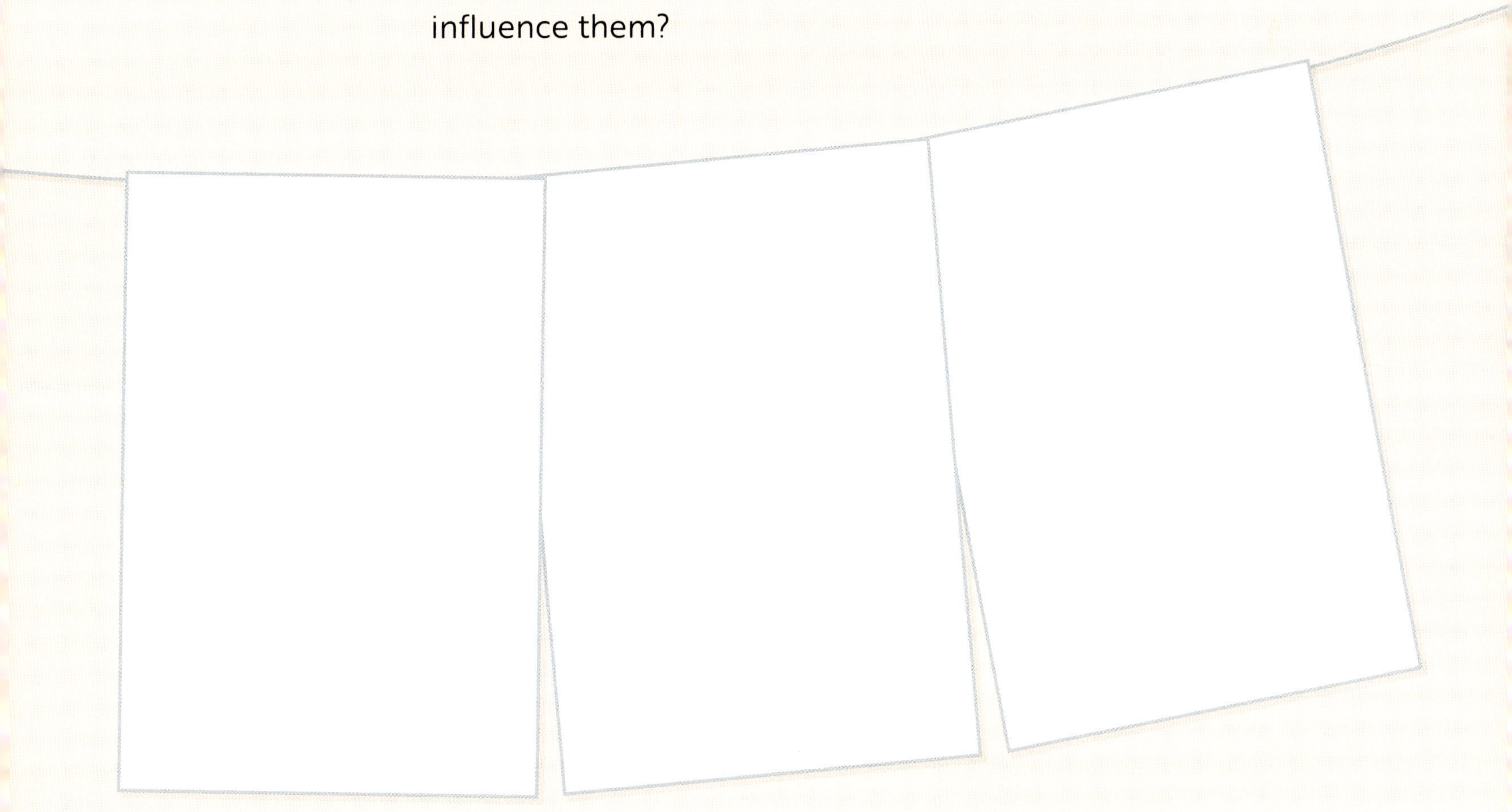

Glossary of terms

Androgynous—used to describe a person with both masculine and feminine traits.

Caesarean section—a procedure used in dangerous births where a pregnant person's belly is cut open to remove the baby inside.

Folk religion—cultural religious practices that are specific to an ethnic group, usually without an organized structure.

Haitian Vodou—a folk religion that developed in Haiti between the 16th and 19th centuries.

Intersex—An umbrella term that refers to people who have sex characteristics outside the typical definitions of male or female.

Klinefelter syndrome—an intersex condition where a person is born with XXY chromosomes instead of XX (female) or XY (male) chromosomes.

Non-binary—an umbrella term referring to people whose gender identity doesn't fit neatly into the definitions of man or woman.

Third gender—a word similar to non-binary that refers to a gender other than man or woman.

Transgender—a word describing someone whose gender identity does not align with their assigned gender at birth.

Two Spirit—an umbrella term used by some Indigenous people to describe a gender traditional to their culture.